Nimble Anointed Words Empower N-AWE

A Book of Poetry

Rosalind Y. Lewis Tompkins

Book cover designed by Sue-Ellen Gardiner

WestBow Press books may be ordered through booksellers or by contacting:

WestBow Press
A Division of Thomas Nelson & Zondervan
1663 Liberty Drive
Bloomington, IN 47403
www.westbowpress.com
1 (866) 928-1240

ISBN: 978-1-5127-1488-3 (sc)
ISBN: 978-1-5127-1489-0 (hc)
ISBN: 978-1-5127-1487-6 (e)

Library of Congress Control Number: 2015916645

Print information available on the last page.

WestBow Press rev. date: 10/16/2015

Other Inspirational Books by Rosalind Y. Tompkins

As Long As There Is Breath In Your Body, There Is Hope

Rare Anointing

You Are Beautiful

What Is It?

Contents

Dedication

I dedicate this book to my granddaughters, Tayla and Mya. May God bless you both with a love for and gift of poetry! I also dedicate this book to poetry lovers everywhere. May the poet in *you* emerge as you read *N-AWE!*

Foreword

It gives me great pleasure to write the foreword for *N-AWE*. I have known Dr. Rosalind Y. Lewis Tompkins for over two decades. She has a powerful testimony of how the Lord Jesus Christ set her free from a life of drugs and alcohol. The good news is that she has been free now for more than thirty years. She has a passion for seeing lives changed by the power of God in fulfilling their destinies.

The Lord has supernaturally graced her with an incredible gift of poetry. She shares practical insights and reveals the heart of the Father, bringing healing and restoration that she received by divine impartation to wounded warriors.

As a mentor, coach, and spiritual father for over three decades, I have met with many people who needed inner healing from secrets located below the surface. This is known as the iceberg theory, which is defined as problems that are located 90 percent below the surface and 10 percent above. These anointed poems go deep below the surface and are personal, powerful, and prophetic. They will be a healing balm to your mind, will, and emotions, resulting in wholeness in every area of your life.

As I read *N-AWE,* it was very difficult to stop reading because of the anointing on these poems. They brought tears to my eyes over and over again and touched the very core of my being. I know that this book will do the same for you as you read her story in poetic form from her adventurous journey in life.

This book is a must read for all those who want their lives to be radically transformed emotionally, relationally, interpersonally, behaviorally, physiologically, psychologically, and spiritually.

As you will read in the pages that follow, poetry can encourage us to make it through tough times, because the words of an anointed poet deposit hope in our hearts. Poetry is spoken from the heart and helps to tell stories in very unique ways.

Get ready for an experience that you will hold dear to your heart from His heart.

I highly commend Dr. Rosalind for this vital contribution to the body of Christ and recommend this book as a powerful resource. I know that these inspired poems will be a tremendous blessing to you as you read them.

Dr. Steven P. Govender, Durban, South Africa
Restoration and Revival Ministries International
Home base: Atlanta, Georgia, United States of America

Acknowledgments

First of all, I give God all the praise, glory, and honor for giving me the gift of writing and the privilege to serve His Word to others through poetry. I thank God for my very supportive and loving husband, Elder Kwame Lewis. You are such a gift and blessing from the Lord! I thank God for Turning Point International Church ministers and members. May God continue to bless and keep you all! Your love, support, prayers, and encouragement keep me lifted. I thank God for my daughter Janar, my mother Louise, and all who inspired the poet in me to come forth. I thank God for my spiritual father, Dr. Steven Govender, and his dear wife Nancy. Last but not least, I thank the Holy Spirit and all of the God-given muses who have inspired me over the years during various seasons of my life.

Introduction

There are tons of books, publications, and articles available about the power and importance of the words that we speak. In the Bible, we find that death and life are in the power of the tongue. In *N-AWE: Nimble Anointed Words Empower,* I will talk about the importance of words that are anointed by God to empower. In essence, anointing is God's empowering and equipping of believers in Christ in order to carry out His work. God empowers us in order for us to accomplish His will and purpose in any given situation and circumstance. In my book *Rare Anointing,* I talk about the kingdom PEDLR (power, endurance, depth, love, relationship) as one who carries God's glory and anointing with power, endurance, depth, love, and relationship. One of the tools of the kingdom PEDLR is anointed words. Anointed words come from the Lord, and He uses them to execute His will.

In order to speak God's words, you have to first be able to hear God's voice and keep the lines of communication open. There has to be a continuous flow of conversation between you and God. Like the river that flows, anointed words flow. It is imperative to hear them and be sensitive to what God is saying. The greatest gift that a kingdom PEDLR possesses is the gift of hearing God's voice. In *N-AWE,* we explore anointed words utilizing my original God-inspired poetry as illustrations.

Words Empower

God used words from the beginning of time to speak the world into existence. He used Jesus, who is the Word of God incarnate, to straighten things out once people messed them up. And He is still using words today. Anointed words are words spoken by the Holy Spirit through us in order to accomplish His purposes. To empower means to be given the authority, allowance, ability, skill, or commissioning to do something; it also means to make stronger or more confident in your abilities to accomplish certain tasks in life. God empowers through both His written words and *rhema*, or spoken words. The Bible says that the Holy Spirit speaks what He hears into the hearts of believers in Christ. Learning to discern the Holy Spirit's voice from all the other voices that speak (i.e., yours, others, the enemy) is essential in speaking anointed words.

I have written and published poems in each of my four books, *As Long As There Is Breath In Your Body, There Is Hope; Rare Anointing; You Are Beautiful;* and *What Is It?* For the remainder of *N-AWE,* I will share several of my published and unpublished original poetry and detail the process that anointed words have to empower. I pray that as you read the poems and hear the backstories behind them, you will see how you can utilize anointed words in your life and ministry.

At the beginning of each chapter, I will identify keys to empowering words. At the end of the book, I will reveal how to use the keys to unlock nimble anointed words inside you that are just waiting to be released.

Chapter 1 Words of Awe

Key to Empowerment: Awe

I have noticed lately that on television and in movies, one person will ask another person to wow him or her. Or they will say, "That didn't wow me." To wow someone essentially means to gain an enthusiastic response from or to thrill. I believe that is what many people spend their time doing in order to be liked on the various social media websites. On YouTube, young people do various hazardous things like jumping from a moving vehicle while someone videotapes them just to wow others and get noticed.

Many times, we inadvertently try to get God to wow us. And while God does move in mysterious ways that cause us to marvel at His power and glory, He does not manifest His power to give us cheap thrills. He desires to transform us into the image of Jesus Christ. Doing that takes more than just wowing; it takes aweing.

Awe is defined as an overwhelming feeling of reverence, admiration, or fear produced by that which is grand, sublime, and extremely powerful. The Bible says that the fear (or awe) of the Lord is the beginning of wisdom. I believe that the reverence that society once had for God and the things of God is no longer there. Because of many scandals involving clergy, priests, and pastors over the last century, we treat God and God's people with disdain. As a result, God and believers in Christ are often the brunt of bad jokes. However, we should never lose our fear, reverence, and awe for our Lord. He is good, no matter what anyone else does or says.

In Awe of You, Lord

I stand in awe of your power and glory;

I love the way you are telling my story.

The things I have suffered and lost and gained—

You have been there through it all and kept me sane, even when I lost my mind.

Every time, you didn't miss a beat but kept it sweet; in the midst of the sour, you became my finest hour.

I stand in awe of your power and glory;

I love the way you are telling my story

Of the things I have done and places I have seen.

You've taken me to places that I only dreamed of seeing;

You let me know it is okay just being in love with you.

I stand in awe of your power and glory;

I love the way you are telling my story—

A story of hope, joy, and sorrow; you let me know that there is always tomorrow.

That's why I can tell others and not be ashamed to always carry your name.

I stand in awe of your power and glory;

I love the way you are telling my story.

Keep on writing the epistles on my heart, and I will continue to do my part and carry the torch to those who will listen

Because I stand in awe of your power and glory, and I love the way you are telling my story.

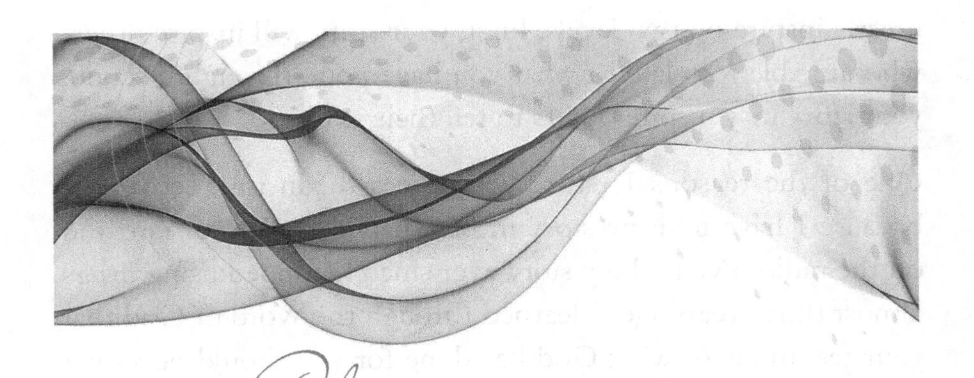

Chapter 2
Words of Stories from the Heart

Key to Empowerment: Knowledge

Have you ever wanted to share something that you felt deeply about but just couldn't find the words to tell it? As a minister and public speaker, I have felt that way on many occasions, primarily as it relates to my story and my addiction and recovery from drugs and alcohol. I was addicted to drugs for twelve years, and I have been free for almost three decades. After a while, the story can get stale if you are not careful. However, I've had the honor of sharing my testimony with many diverse groups in America and around the world. Each time, I feel as though it was the first time, because I learned how to use anointed words to empower.

The first key to using anointed words is having knowledge about your audience and subject matter. You must know what to say and when and how to say it. This requires awareness, which begins with self-awareness. You know your story better than anyone else because you have lived it. Telling your story with authenticity can greatly inspire on two levels. First, your story will inspire others who are able to relate to what you have gone through. Second, your story may inspire others to tell their stories.

One of the reasons I have been successful in my recovery is because I have told my story in newspapers, on television, and on the radio. I've told my story ever since I stopped using drugs almost thirty years ago. I learned through the Word of God that your testimony of what God has done for you should never get old or become lukewarm, because God deserves better. He has done great things. There are always people who need to hear what you have gone through in order to build their faith for what they are experiencing.

When speaking anointed words, it's important to speak from the heart. Heartfelt words and emotions go deeper than words spoken only from the head or intellect. Poetry is spoken from the heart and helps to tell stories in unique ways.

Below, I share several of my poems that help to tell my story. On a recent trip to South Africa, I used these poems to minister during a crusade and saw miraculous results. Wherever I share these and other poems, people are touched to the core of their beings in tremendous ways that I will never forget.

I wrote "Tears" years ago when I was still in college. Right before I got pregnant with Janar, I was trying to change my life and get right with the Lord. I had no idea of the things that I would eventually do in ministry through Mothers in Crisis. I did not know I would impact thousands of women and families caught up in the vicious cycle of addiction. I now know that the encounter with the Lord that I share in "Tears" was the beginning of me receiving the Lord's burden.

Tears

As I sat in my usual morning spot deep in the woods, meditating upon the Lord, I prayed for my brothers and sisters. The longer I prayed, the deeper my burden became. Gradually, tears began to roll down my face. My eyes were swollen shut as I cried in a loud voice unto the Lord. My tears engulfed me. They surrounded me in prayer. Only it was not just my tears, for it had started to rain very hard. The rain was icy cold when it hit my face and mingled with my tears. A tiny vapor of steam rose and evaporated. Hard and steady was the rain. Heavy and loud was my cry.

Refreshing yet sad, cleansing yet sorrowful was the rain as it poured.

The Lord is a compassionate God. He hears our cries and feels our hurts. He mourns when we mourn, and He will lift us up and place us where He would have us to be. Trust in the Lord thy God always. That morning, the Lord and I cried.

"My Baby Girl" tells the story of how my daughter helped me to get off of drugs. In the poem, I talk about how I lived before she came along and how she helped me to get closer to God.

My Baby Girl

When you came into my world, my life was a mess, and you know that!

You showed up on the scene, all sparkling and clean.

You were just what I needed to help me really believe that

It was time to take stock of my life.

You see, prior to your arrival, I was living like a wild girl, caught in the cycle of addiction.

Baby girl, you taught me conviction!

All of sudden, I had another to think about other than myself.

It was through my love for you that Christ's love finally shined through the muck and mire of my life.

Love for my baby girl!

You changed my world with one smile and a cry;

Even the diapers that I would dry helped me to see life through different eyes.

I had purpose and destiny lying in my lap before me

As I dreamed of you and I taking life by storm

While wrapped in the capable arms of our Father who is in heaven.

So as you live your life and grow, please always know that I was your first life's mission.

Mission accomplished, baby girl.

Thank you for changing my world!

"Rare Anointing" is a poem that I wrote to talk about the significance of pain and suffering and how God uses them to empower us to help others who are going through tough times.

Rare Anointing

"It's oh so special, oh so sweet,"

Crowned with glory from head to feet.

Some may say, "How'd you get that way?"

Well, I've been through the fire, and I been through the rain;

I've been so confused until I didn't even know my own name.

I been up to heaven, and yes, I've been down to hell;

I've seen and heard things that I dare not tell.

I wondered, waited, and anticipated,

Looking intently to be emancipated from the trials and tribulations that I co-created only to find a new state of mind when I realized that it was all for a purpose.

You see, in order to produce the wine, the grapes must be crushed, and in order to produce the oil, the olives must be pressed, and in order to produce the anointing, I must confess:

Something had to die!

Death is painful at its best.

But through the pain, I learned to rest and

Trust the Lord through each and every test.

Out of the suffering and out of the pain, I heard the Lord Jesus calling my name. He said, "Rosalind, come forth; I'm here for you. There is something for you to do. The blind must see, the dumb must talk, the deaf must hear, and the lame must walk."

I learned a valuable lesson that I want to share with you.

No matter what you may be going through—no matter how painful, haunting, daunting, or taunting it may be—

Just remember, it is producing a rare anointing to set the captives free!

I shared the next poem, "Transformation," in many different settings. But the occasion that really stands out is when I shared it with grade school students in the Bahamas as part of the Cruise for a Cause outreach. "Transformation" tells the story of a caterpillar changing into a butterfly. It's simple and can be fun to share, but the message is very deep. It talks about how the caterpillar sees inside that she is more than what she appears to be, and through that process, the transformation takes place. The poem then likens it to the transformation process of believers in Christ. It's a fun poem, and I often get lots of smiles and laughter as the message goes down. This is fine with me, because anointed words go deep and produce a range of emotions, including tears and laughter.

Transformation

The caterpillar wonders why she can't fly,

Crawling around with her head hanging down, wearing a frown.

Inside, she sees wings like none she's ever seen,

Flying high through the sky among the trees.

But in reality, day after day, she crawls around, dodging birds of prey.

But inside she sees wings like none she's ever seen,

Flying high through the sky among the trees.

One day, she believes as she sees that the wings belong to her.

She pictures herself flying, and a process begins trying to make her become what she was born to be.

The process of transformation is finally taking her off the ground and into the trees,

Flying high through the sky with wings like none she's ever seen.

But now she possesses and her soul caresses life as it is supposed to be—

No more crawling around with her head hanging down, wearing a frown;

She now has her wings to fly high through the sky, way up in the trees!

You may be like that caterpillar, living your life crawling around with your head hanging down, wearing a frown.

Jesus came to give you your wings so you too can fly high through the sky, way up in the trees.

Look inside, where Christ resides, and see the new creation that you were born again to be;

Allow the process of transformation to begin taking you off the ground and into the trees,

Flying high in the Spirit with wings like none you've ever seen.

But now you possess and your soul can caress life and that more abundantly!

Chapter 3
Words of Encouragement

Key to Empowerment: Hope

Hope is a powerful force that can propel you to continue to try even when the going gets tough. One of the ways that we are infused with hope is through anointed words. Anointed words encourage us to hope and trust God.

I am known for my trademarked saying, "As long as there is breath in your body, there is hope." This is also the title of my first book, in which I share how I went through the hellhole of crack cocaine addiction and made it out by the grace of God. In the book, I share how I came out of my addiction with eight pearls of wisdom. One pearl is the power of hope.

I will never forget when I first adopted this saying. I was working in the social work field with drug- and alcohol-addicted women in several rural counties, trying to get them into treatment. My daughter was just a baby, and after working all day, I came home and took care of her. As a single parent, this was not easy. I would sit and pray after putting Janar to bed for the night. On one particular night after a very exhausting day, I began to cry out to the Lord. I said something like, "What's the use running after these women trying to get them help? They just keep on doing the same thing anyway."

While I prayed, the Lord said to me in a very still, small voice, "As long as there is breath in your body, there is hope." I immediately felt peace come and the burden lift. After that, every time I felt overwhelmed by something the women that I worked with did, I would say, "As long as there is breath in your body, there is hope." I eventually trademarked the saying with the US Patent Office and used it as a tagline for many of the local public service announcements that I wrote and appeared in over a ten-year period.

I wrote "Where Is Hope?" to answer the question that I received on many occasions while ministering in jails and prisons where I shared my testimony of addiction and deliverance. I would tell the ladies to remember, "As long as there is breath in your body, there is hope." Inevitably, someone would say something like, "I am going through hell right now, and I don't see any hope; where is this hope that you are talking about?"

I was privileged to share this poem on the steps of the Kigali Genocide Memorial Centre in Rwanda, Africa. I had just toured the museum and witnessed thousands upon thousands of skulls of children and adults killed during the genocide in Rwanda. I was asked to share a poem as I left the museum with my group. I stood on the steps, while armed guards stood on top of the building with big rifles. I looked up to heaven and then shared this poem with the small group that gathered around me.

Where Is Hope?

Hope is found in the breath that I breathe,

In the stars in the sky, and in the cool of the breeze.

Hope is found in a baby's cry or tears rolling down the eye

Of one who knows that every good thing flows from the heart of God.

Hope is found in the birds that sing, in the grass as it grows,

In the smell of a rose, in the dew as it settles upon the ground.

Hope can be found in the middle of pain, in the streets of frustration,

And in the home of the name that is above every name!

Hope is found when you near the name, think the name, or say the name—

It's all the same

Because Jesus *is hope!*

I wrote "You Are Beautiful"—which is also the title of one of my books—primarily for my daughter Janar, who was a sophomore in college. She was and is gorgeous, but she could not see it. I understood completely because I used to feel the same way until I realized that true beauty comes from within. It is released through your relationship with Christ. I have ministered this poem to countless women during inner beauty seminars to help them unlock their beauty from within.

You Are Beautiful

Beauty resides in the hearts of those who seek to find it.

I am often reminded of how it eludes those who think it is hidden

When truth be told, it is all around us, waiting to be uncovered and discovered from within.

Beauty is present to bring pleasure that we can treasure throughout the ages as we turn the pages of our lives.

Why does beauty seem to hide behind images that are fleeting and fading and often wading in hypocrisy and lies?

It is often disguised by what appears to be real.

The only problem is that when it is captured, it leaves you hollow and full of sorrow and regret.

Beauty that is only skin deep is not beauty at all, because true beauty is found well below the surface, and it resides in the very core of one's soul.

Truth be told, beauty that is felt is beauty that is seen, and true beauty is found in everything.

It is in the trees, in the sky, and especially in the eyes of those filled with God's presence.

Beauty must be cherished and pampered, loved and acknowledged, or it will be malnourished and forget its purpose and die a slow death.

Beauty is as beauty does, because life is not only measured by how you look, but by who you are and by what you do. And I must say to you that *you are beautiful!*

I wrote "You've Got to Have It" for my book *What Is It?* This poem encourages one to find purpose and destiny by asking questions that many who are searching for meaning in life can relate to. "You've Got to Have It" encourages you to step out of the proverbial boat in order to fulfill your life's purpose.

You've Got to Have It

What is it that wakes you up from the inside out?

What is it that screams in silence but comes out as a shout that can only be heard by you and God?

What is it that calls to you when your heart is still and tickles your soul while strengthening your will?

That's the *it* that can be fulfilled when you realize that

You've got to have your life enhanced.

So take a chance

To understand that there's more in store

For those willing to risk it all

And seek to find what's been left behind

But hidden deep inside.

Come take a ride with me,

Because your journey awaits; your destiny is calling. Your purpose is ripe,

So take a bite of the things you desire.

I know you want to go higher and have a ball

Because you've got to have *it,* and you can have *it* all.

Prayer is an intricate part of the life of a believer in Christ. I love to pray, and over the years, I have found creative ways to pray even with my eyes. The poem "Prayer" captures moments of intimate prayer that I have experienced and the hope that prayer brings.

Prayer

Now I lay me down to pray.

I pray you will help me find a way

To do your will each and every day;

Then I won't give up and go astray.

I wish I might, I wish I may

Love you more than words can say.

When I run out of words to say,

It is with my eyes that I pray as I behold beauty and glory.

I hear the story of how you came for one such as me.

God is saying, "As you sat praying, I heard the cry of your heart.

I like what I hear; therefore, I draw near to manifest my peace and grace.

The more I am present, the pain is lessened, and the knowledge of hope bursts through."

Chapter 4 Words of Life & Times

Key to Empowerment: Resilience

There are many ways to capture, express, and relate seasons and occurrences in life. Many people write journals and blogs, take photos, or paint in order to capture the heart of a particular moment in time. These moments are often based upon the collective experiences of a people or society. I write poetry.

The poems that I share in this chapter were all written specifically to capture a particular sentiment based upon what was happening at the time. These poems helped me to share how I felt about what was happening. Nimble anointed words are able to succinctly and powerfully sum up the pathos of particular situations that occur in life. They help make sense out of the senseless while encouraging and empowering others to feel the emotions of a particular moment in time. Poetry can inspire us to make it through tough times, because the words of an anointed poet deposit hope in our hearts.

I was watching *The Oprah Winfrey Show* several years ago around the time when genocide was taking place in Rwanda. As Oprah and a guest talked about what was happening, I was outraged. I remember praying and asking God what I could do to help. I took a nap, and when I woke up, He gave me the poem "Genocide." I had no idea that I would one day visit Rwanda.

Genocide

Children dying,

Mothers crying.

Women raped—

No escape.

Where to hide?

It's genocide!

Jesus died,

Shed His blood,

Rose again

So we could win

Against all sin!

Help is coming:

Letter-writing,

Outraged sighing—

What to do?

It's up to you!

Praying and fasting,

Listening and speaking—

We won't stop until someone's keeping

Watch over the children of the world.

God bless the children!

I wrote "I Cannot Be Shaken" in 2008 while the United States went through a major economic downturn. I, like many others, lost most of my income because of the slow economy. As executive director of my nonprofit organization, Mothers In Crisis, I wrote grants for funding our programs. When the economy crashed, the grants dried up. I ended up losing my job and my home. I was also going through a divorce, and I had just found out that my daughter, who was nineteen years old at the time, was pregnant. In the midst of all the things that were being shaken in my life, I realized that my relationship with the Lord Jesus Christ is greater than anything that I lost or experienced at the time.

I Cannot Be Shaken

There is a quaking going on—if I'm not mistaken, everything around is being shaken;

People losing homes right and left,

Banking institutions crumbling fast,

Gas prices up and down, and Wall Street crashed.

Job security is a thing of the past!

There is a quaking going on—if I'm not mistaken, everything around is being shaken;

Husbands and wives on the split,

War going on endlessly,

Teenagers having sex recklessly,

People wondering how this could be.

Living in the twenty-first century,

Life was supposed to be about unity.

Instead, we spent time acquiring things:

Houses, cars, and diamond rings.

We just wanted to be living large—

The only problem is who's in charge.

What we didn't really know

Is that it is the creditors that we owe.

Now this whole thing is about to blow

Like a big fat fiery volcano!

There is a quaking going on—if I'm not mistaken, everything around is being shaken;

Things that cannot be shaken are holding on.

The kingdom of God is still growing strong.

I cannot be shaken!

In February 2012, Trayvon Martin, a seventeen-year-old black youth, was shot and killed by a vigilante named George Zimmerman in Sanford, Florida. In July 2014, Eric Garner, a forty-three-year-old black man, was choked to death my NYPD officers while saying, "I can't breathe." In August 2014, an eighteen-year-old black young man, Michael Brown, was shot and killed by a police officer in Ferguson, Missouri. In April 2015, Freddie Gray died of an unexplained spinal cord injury while in police custody. On April 27, 2015, Baltimore, Maryland went up in flames with rioting. These were some of the incidents that inspired me to write this poem.

Life Goes On

The telephone is ringing.

The sun is shining;

The wind is blowing.

Life goes on—

The television is blaring, glaring, and I sit staring at images of a war-torn nation.

The only problem is, we are not at war, or are we?

Life goes on—

The children are playing;

The cars are traveling to and fro.

I wonder where they are going, and do they know that we are at war,

A war from within?

The enemy that we fight day and night—

Each other, no compassion for a sister or a brother in pain; what a shame.

Life goes on—

The stores are selling goods and wares;

We buy our stuff, and it seems like nobody cares.

Life goes on—

Our black men are trying, dying, while crying,

"I can't breathe!"

No, not a noose this time—

Called into a life of crime or maybe just walking the line.

Life goes on—

The protectors of society are on their beat.

"Murder, murder!" we cry in the streets.

And life goes on.

I was born in Pensacola, Florida and then moved to Tallahassee for college. I have lived here for most of my life. As such, I am used to hurricanes hitting the state of Florida. But in 2005, several hurricanes hit Florida back to back, including Hurricane Katrina. It was also a period of time when gas prices were extremely high, and many people were giving up hope. I wrote "I Believe in Miracles" and shared it on my poetry CD, *Poems of Life*. I received feedback from several people who said this poem really blessed them and reminded them to keep the faith.

I Believe in Miracles

In this day and age of skepticism,

Racism, materialism, sexism, and atheism,

I believe in miracles!

In this day and age of haters, players,

Cocaine, hurricanes, gas prices off the chain,

I still believe in miracles!

You see, it started with a miracle when Jesus was conceived,

And the miracles continued the moment I believed

That there was a way out of darkness and the hell that I was in—

The moment I was born again and made Jesus my friend.

The light was turned on, so no matter what is going on,

I believe in miracles!

I wrote "Life Is like a Turtle" during a time of slow growth in my life. I was waiting on my ministry to come into fruition, but it seemed to take forever. I also felt as though I was in hiding, just waiting for God to call me out and reveal me to the nations. This particular poem was not written based upon any outward social or societal occurrences in life but inner times of struggle and turmoil.

Life Is like a Turtle

Life is like a turtle: it takes its own sweet time.

It walks along slowly, wearing its burdens on its back;

It hides in its shell from any future attack.

It stops and goes inside to hide from the harsh realities of this world.

It comes out cautiously, peeping from behind.

It begins its journey again, taking one step at a time,

Looking around to see if the coast is clear.

Or perhaps it will hear a voice sweetly saying, "Come out!"

Life is a like a turtle; it takes its own sweet time,

And I am like a turtle, hiding inside until the coast is clear.

I'll know when I hear the voice that is oh so dear calling me out.

Sweetly, I'll hear the voice of the one I love telling me to continue on my journey.

Life is like a turtle; it takes its own sweet time.

It walks along slowly, wearing its burdens on its back;

It hides in its shell from any future attack.

Chapter 5
Words of Dreams & Visions

Keys to Empowerment: Dream, Dream Big, and Dream Again

Proverbs 29:18 says, "Where *there is* no vision, the people perish." (KJV) This is very true. I have found that in order to move forward in life, you must have an inner picture of what you desire to achieve. These inner pictures are visions that come through dreams, whether you are asleep or awake. Anointed words are like cameras that capture and memorialize the dreams and visions that we have in order to give them life. The following poems depict moments in my life when I dreamed. I have shared these particular poems in many settings where people were able to see the dreams and join me in them.

"Grab the Wind" came to me one day while I was driving with my hand stuck up through the sunroof. The wind was blowing my hand, and I tried to grab it and hold on to it. I made a fist with the wind in my hand, but by the time I got home and opened my hand, I realized the folly of trying to hold on to the wind. In 2014, I shared this poem at the National Faith Symposium for the state of Florida. I likened grabbing the wind to doing something extremely difficult. I then shared steps to grabbing the wind based upon the eight pearls of wisdom that are found in my first book, *As Long aAs There Is Breath iIn Your Body, There Is Hope.* I shared how I grabbed the wind on three major occasions in my life. The first time was when I stopped using drugs almost thirty years ago and remained clean and sober for all these years. The second time I grabbed the wind was when I started Mothers In Crisis in 1991. The third time I grabbed the wind, I met my husband through eHarmony and married him within six months.

Grab the Wind

I grabbed the wind in the palm of my hand.

I made a fist and held it real tight;

I kept it that way for most of the night.

Curiosity got the best of me, and I decided to take a peek and see what the wind looked like as it sat in my hand.

I opened my hand very slowly, one finger at a time;

I looked for the wind, but the wind I couldn't find.

For as I opened my hand, the wind fled, *whoosh,* to the sky;

It left my grasp in the blink of an eye.

I didn't mind, you see, because I came to understand that not many people can honestly say, "I held the wind in the palm of my hand!"

The power I felt for that brief moment made me cry to think that I, a mere mortal, could grab the wind.

There was a season in my life when I went walking for hours at a time in the state forest. On one such occasion, as I sat by a lake deep in the heart of the woods, I heard "Destiny's Calling." It came to me so vividly that I could actually see, hear, and feel it. I have shared this poem over the years to countless people who have seen and felt it as well. For me, "Destiny's Calling" resonates on a personal level of faith. I believe that God has a purpose, plan, and destiny for us all, and we just have to hear and obey the call.

Destiny's Calling

Look through the door of infinity and see destiny calling.

Smell the wind as it tickles your nose and blows open the door.

Walk into the place where time and space cease to be—destiny is waiting patiently.

Water falls and engulfs the air; cries of laughter are everywhere—

Singing and dancing, walking and prancing.

"Live life to the fullest," destiny is saying.

"No time for worry, doubt, or fear; it's time for love and living here."

Hours pass that seem like minutes floating on a cloud.

Time is spent, and the sun is no more.

Hesitantly, I walk back through the door of infinity.

I glance back as destiny winks and blows a kiss.

With tears and a smile, I know I will miss this place.

Destiny is calling. Can't you hear?

Walk into the place where time and space cease to be. Destiny is waiting patiently.

"In My Mind's Eye" is a short poem that I wrote while traveling on an airplane. Through my vivid imagination, God spoke to me and showed me that there are no limits or boundaries that can hold me back. Over the years, I have shared this poem primarily with children to encourage them to keep growing tall in every area of their lives, because there are no limits in God.

In My Mind's Eye

As I sat looking out of the window of an airplane, in my mind's eye, I saw trees.

I saw the tops of pines, palms, and oak trees standing tall through the clouds.

As I considered such an unusual sign, a thought occurred to me.

If trees can grow beyond their limitations and continue to grow taller and taller through the clouds, then why can't I?

As a matter of fact, I think I will grow taller and taller, beyond limitations and expectations, through the clouds, way up high to the heavens—in my mind's eye.

I used to live in a home that was in the heart of the city but located across the street from a thickly wooded area that had lots of trees and untouched land. It was home to many owls and other animals that you normally see out in the woods. "Evil Is Lurking" is a poem that I wrote based upon one of many annoying encounters with the owls in my former neighborhood. The owls came to symbolize evil for me because of my eerie experiences with them, especially in the middle of the night.

Evil Is Lurking

In the wee hours of the morning, the owls gather together,

Howling, clucking, and hooting praises to their god—

Sounds so near but yet so far.

Sleep is arrested, and my patience is tested by the

Howling, clucking, and hooting of the owls.

I bind the forces that sent the owls to my lair,

Because I know who is lurking there.

The moment of truth comes when I join the symphony of

Howling, clucking, and hooting of the owls

By pushing my car's panic button.

My driving machine now enters the scene and begins

Honking, blinking, and blowing.

Suddenly, out of nowhere, silence fills the air.

No more howling, clucking, and hooting of the owls.

I say goodnight as I take a flight into dream world,

And behold, right before my subconscious eyes, are the owls.

"Dream Again" is one of my favorite poems because it gives you a sense of hope. I have shared this poem in jails and prisons, churches, conferences, and community events with diverse groups of people all around the world. It's a call to action that encourages people to put their dreams and visions into action in order to make this world a better place to live. I wrote "Dream Again" during a transitional season in my life when I saw where I wanted to go but knew I had to leave where I was in order to get there.

Dream Again

I had a dream last night, but it didn't last long.

In the dream, I was singing a song

About how in life, things can go wrong—

But even then, there is a chance to go on.

I had a dream last night about what love looked like,

And in the dream, I thought about the plight of men and women

Caught up in a daze, purple haze, eyes all glazed, looking half-crazed,

Walking and wandering through life unfazed by all of the chaos and sin all around, looking for love in a world turned upside down.

I had a dream last night, but something had changed.

The tables had turned, and inside, my head burned with the awareness and knowledge that life is for living and love is for loving and songs are for singing—and in the midst of it all, my alarm clock started ringing.

I arose from my bed, shook my head, and thought about the things that I had reaped—and then it dawned on me that I wasn't really asleep!

For the first time in my life, my eyes were wide opened, and I was aware and awake to the things that make life worth living and time worth giving to the things that bring release and offer peace.

So whether awake or asleep, dream of a life filled with songs for the soul and love that makes whole whatever is broken.

Dream of hope and joy for better days ahead;

And when you dream, get out of your bed and bring to reality the things that were said.

Dream again.

Chapter 6 Words of Ministry

Key to Empowerment: Servant's Heart

Ministry is essentially serving the Word of God and the Holy Spirit. This can be done through helping others in various ways, whether feeding the hungry, providing encouragement to the downtrodden, praying for the sick, or preaching a sermon. It all comes back to the place of service.

I have ministered using all of my poetry, and I find that it is a great way to share the good news of Christ because the words go straight into listeners' hearts. As a result, I have encountered many reactions from the poems that I share, from tears to goosebumps, laughter, and shaking. I believe the words of the poems are anointed by God to release His Spirit into the hearts of those who are open.

"Destiny Is Fulfilled" is a poem of great depth. It gets to the heart of the various trials and tribulations many people experience. It reminds us that we have greatness on the inside and can fulfill the destiny that God has for each of us. I shared "Destiny Is Fulfilled" with a young lady who had experienced much pain and abuse growing up. As a result, she began cutting herself in order to relieve pain that she felt inside. When I read "Destiny Is Fulfilled" to her, she began to cry and tremble. She related to the poem on a deep level and received the message. It blesses me tremendously to see the results of anointed words that God uses to minster to and comfort others on such a visceral level.

Destiny Is Fulfilled

The time has come, and the time is now.

You have been looking and searching because you didn't know how you were going to make it; you just couldn't take it.

The trials and tribulations of life got you down.

It got so bad until you thought you would drown in your own blood; but like a flood, the Spirit lifted up a standard and brought you through it.

Although you couldn't see it, you made it to it—the place of destiny.

You heard the call and had to dream again after the fall, because after all, you believed inside that you are more than your problems and more than your pain.

You are much more than that; but all the same, you had to know and do the Father's will, because that is the way that destiny is fulfilled!

Who you are is who you will be; your purpose in life lies within.

Deep inside, you see you can win because greatness is there, and that is who you are.

When you trust in Jesus, then you can go far, high above the clouds, and sit upon a star and look down over your problems and say, "Peace; be still.

Because from where I'm sitting, destiny is fulfilled!"

I have ministered the poem "In the Midst of It All" on many occasions, but one in particular really stands out for me. It was at a funeral of a young man who had been shot to death while robbing a convenience store. This young man had been part of the youth programs of Mothers In Crisis and was the same age as my daughter. He ended up spending time in prison for another robbery. When he got out, he attempted to rob the store where he was killed. It was a tragic loss to his family and friends. Although I was no longer his pastor, I loved him as a son. When I shared this poem at the funeral, it brought a sense of awareness to the fact that Jesus was there to comfort and heal.

In the Midst of It All

As you live your life, going through trials and tests,

There are some things that can cause you great stress.

They come to make you want to give up;

They zap your energy and empty your cup.

But in the midst of it all, you can stand tall!

In the midst of it all, on Him you must call;

He will hear and answer your cry.

Why don't you just try?

Even if you have had a fall;

He is right there with you in the midst of it all,

Waiting on your call.

Call on Jesus. Don't be like King Saul who went to the witch and dug a great ditch into which he did fall!

Seek the Lord; give Him a call, because He is right there with you in the midst of it all!

I ministered at an outdoor revival held at a community center in a very impoverished community several years ago. The message that I shared was about letting go and letting God break every chain. As I shared this message, a young lady ran out of her home and came to the event crying uncontrollably. She reeked of alcohol. We prayed for her in Jesus' name, and she immediately sobered up. I told her to "Let It Go."

Let It Go

There is a power that can break every yoke;

This power that I'm talking about is not a joke.

So many people don't believe or know that life is only lived when you truly let go.

Let it flow; let it go so you can grow.

Many people living don't know who they are;

They don't know that they can go far. But in order to do that, you have to know the name.

The name that I'm talking about can break every chain and take away the shame.

Jesus is His name; let Him break every chain!

When you trust in Jesus, then you can break every chain. When you call upon His name, He takes away the pain; He takes away the shame and gives you hope so you can cope.

There is a power that can break every yoke;

This power that I'm talking about is not a joke.

The chains of bondage, poverty, disease, and oppression must go.

Let it flow; let it go so you can grow.

I was struggling in an area of my life when the poem "Temptation" came to me. The words ministered to me. I have since used them to minister to countless others who battle areas of weakness.

Temptation

And I said, "Lord, deliver me.

I wish I could be like that tree,

Standing tall with no feelings at all!"

But you gently said to me, "If you were indeed like that tree,

Then there'd be no need for me!

Take it easy, fast, and pray; remember me in all you do and say.

It takes faith and patience to run this race, and don't forget, my grace is sufficient.

For when you are weak, I am strong. I'm here to help when things go wrong.

Take the time to renew your mind.

Submit your will and your body too;

Then you will receive power to make it through

Any and all temptations that come to you.

Submit to me; resist the Devil, and he will flee."

And I said, "Lord, thank you much.

I now receive your touch, your love, your strength, and your grace.

I now have power to run this race.

For when I am weak, you are strong.

Your power helps me to carry on!"

I have used the short poem "Blessings" to minister at my church on various occasions. This poem reiterates how the Lord's blessings are like waterfalls continually flowing. That's precisely how the Lord blesses us to a thousand generations. Many of my members know this particular poem by heart, and they recite it often.

Blessings

The blessings of God are not dripping and dropping,

But flowing like a river and never stopping.

The blessings of God are not dripping and dropping,

But flowing like a river and never stopping.

I said, The blessings of God are not dripping and dropping,

But flowing like a river and never stopping!

Chapter 7 Words of Inspiration

Key to Empowerment: Creativity

Inspiration is essentially the process of being mentally stimulated to do or feel something creative. In order for the right words to come, you must be inspired either externally or internally. Nature is a wonderful place to be inspired. It is where I write many of my poems. It's as though the beauty of nature connects with the beauty of God from within me. This results in anointed words coming out of me. I wrote all of the poems in this chapter while experiencing the intoxicating power of nature—whether deep in the heart of the woods, by a lake, looking at the sand on the desert, or at the beach, watching the waves.

Several years ago, I traveled to Nevada for a poetry contest. As the airplane neared our destination, I looked out of the window and saw the vast desert below. I saw miles and miles of sand. I was blessed, as this was the first time in my life that I had seen the desert this close. As I looked out the window, I begin to think about how just the other day, I was at the beach in San Destin, Florida. As a native Floridian, I love the beach and go as often as possible. As my mind and spirit contrasted the desert and ocean, I wrote this poem, "Water and Sand."

Water and Sand

From the ocean to the desert, God made this great land.

He's given us the knowledge and wisdom to understand

It's not about houses, cars, or material things,

But it's all about love and the hope that brings

For new life and possibilities that expand with each and every day.

From the sky to the sea, from the forest to you and me, there is an

Ocean, there is a desert, and there are mountains and valleys.

Clear as the sky on a warm summer's day,

Sweet as the mango ripened in the sun,

Hard as the pearl enclosed in the oyster,

Grand as the mind set on finding answers

Is the life filled with oceans and deserts!

I love the ocean and the sound of water. One day, I was at my favorite beach during a storm. As the wind blew, the waves crashed against the seashore, and the rain poured, I heard the poem "Powerful."

Powerful

Crushing, rushing majesty—the voice of the Lord speaks.

From the depth of the sea, the ocean is calling me to a place that I have never been.

The power of the ocean surrounds me.

Crushing, rushing majesty—the voice of the Lord speaks.

Inside of me, I hear the call of the sea; the ocean sings a melody of powerful possibilities.

I rock, I sway, and I'm lulled away as an infant in a cradle or a baby in the womb.

I am engulfed by the sea; the ocean speaks to me.

Crushing, rushing majesty; the voice of the Lord speaks!

As I walked into the heart of the woods to spend time with the Lord and experience the quietness and stillness of His presence, I wrote the poems "Greatness," "Inside Out," "Harmony," and "Vapor."

It is in His presence that greatness is revealed, and it is under the banner of His glory that greatness is fulfilled.

Greatness

Is this not the place where greatness begins?

Is this not the place where greatness ends?

Yes, this is the place where greatness begins, and this is the place where greatness ends.

In His presence, the connection is made that lights the temple and lets up the shade; but this is also the place where the glory of God outshines every other light.

Yes, this is the place where greatness begins, and this is the place where greatness ends—in His presence.

Inside Out

Life in you, life through you—

I take a ride and journey inside to the place that never ends;

It just begins and begins and begins.

Tears are flowing, never knowing where they start or end, but realizing that it is from within that the river flows outward toward the gate of eternity.

Caught up in time, hearing the rhyme of creation as it praises the one who gives life.

In the midst of it all, I receive a call from the one who makes me laugh in the middle of tears.

Harmony

The blackbird calls a sound of passion and praise,

An orchestra of sounds both near and far:

Buzzing, singing, blowing, flowing, chirping.

Ducks are flying;

All are trying to express in the language they have been given,

Just as I try and try to express my love, adoration, and thanks

To the one who conducts it all!

Vapor

Man and his boat,

Staying afloat

As the wind blows hard and the trees sway,

Zips past.

Won't last,

Out of gas—

Time to go

For sure!

Chapter 8 Words of Declaration

Key to Empowerment: Awareness

Proverbs 18:21 says, "Death and life *are* in the power of the tongue", (KJV) or the words that we speak. I believe this to be true. Anointed words bring life and release God's power into the hearts of those who are open to receive them. We need to declare not only positive words, but also words that come from the heart and mouth of God over our children and ourselves. They don't have to be big, fancy words to make an impact, but they do have to reveal truth in order to be effective.

"I Am the Joy" is a poem that is based upon Hebrews 12:1, where Jesus says that it was for the joy that was set before Him that He endured the cross, despising the shame. I wrote about the power of joy as it relates to pain and suffering in my book *Rare Anointing* and included this poem. I have ministered "I Am the Joy" to a wide variety of audiences from the USA to South Africa to Turkey. Every time that I have shared this poem, people are able to relate and understand that they are the joy or the reason Jesus died on the cross and rose again on the third day.

I Am the Joy

When I look into the mirror, tell me—what do I see?

The reflection of the glory staring back at me!

The essence of Christ is who I see,

And I realize that it is no longer me but we.

For I am the joy that was set before my Lord

As He hung, bled, and died on the cross for my sins.

Creation cried and thought it was the end.

But today, I know that it didn't end but begin,

For I am the joy!

As I go throughout my day burdened by the weight of the world,

I stop and realize, as I look into His eyes, that I am the joy!

I am the one who He saw and decided to stay on that cross so that I wouldn't be lost.

I am the joy, and because I am, I can laugh and not cry, smile and not frown, live and not die!

I can continue to try and try to reach the goal of my soul being with my Savior.

Every day, it carries me along the way just to know that I am the joy!

I wrote the poetic utterance "Drugs Steal, and Violence Kills" as part of a Mothers In Crisis antidrug and antiviolence campaign. It was used in several local public service announcements with tremendous results. Parents of children told us how their kids repeated the words, which really caught on and got down in their hearts. One parent said that her son repeated this poem day and night!

Drugs Steal, and Violence Kills

Drugs steal, and violence kills,

So don't do drugs or use your fist,

But use your brain and remember this:

Drugs steal, and violence kills!

Drugs steal, and violence kills!

Drugs steal, and violence kills!

Often when we experience problems in life, it is easy to blame others for our troubles. I have seen this happen over the years while helping the women of Mothers In Crisis. They often blamed others for their drug problems or for losing their children. I used to do that as well until one day, I took a good look in the mirror and did a self-assessment. I was both dismayed and delighted when I realized that I was the problem. I was dismayed because I had to take responsibility for my actions and the consequences of them. I was delighted because if I was the problem, then that meant I could fix it, because the only person who you can truly change is yourself.

Ene-Me

I searched for the enemy. I looked as far as my eyes could see; I looked and I looked and I looked. I searched for the enemy. I looked as far as my eyes could see; I looked and I looked and I looked. I searched for the enemy. I looked as far as my eyes could see; I looked and I looked and I looked. I searched for the enemy. I looked as far as my eyes could see, until I finally realized that the enemy was *me!*

The poem "Freedom Maker" was inspired by a Blog Talk internet radio show that I cohosted called *Freedom Makers*. Another pastor and I spoke about relevant issues from the standpoint of freedom in Christ Jesus. I thought about how the Lord delivered me from drugs and alcohol almost thirty years ago and healed my mind from the psychotic episodes that I talk about in my book *As Long aAs There Is Breath iIn Your Body, There Is Hope*. Since my deliverance, I have walked in freedom and helped countless others to become free in Christ.

Freedom Maker

To be free for me is to see beyond the things that are right in front of my eyes, blocking the view of the true life that is hidden in Christ, my Lord.

To be free for me is to remember the chains that had me deranged, changed into something that was not real but made to feel less than, incomplete, unless medicated to the point of oblivion. Thank God for freedom that came just in time.

To be free for me is to know that no matter how far I go or how long I stay, there is always another day, a new way for me to reveal the person that I was intended to be throughout eternity. That person is me. Free, freedom, freed, freedom maker, that's me—*free!*

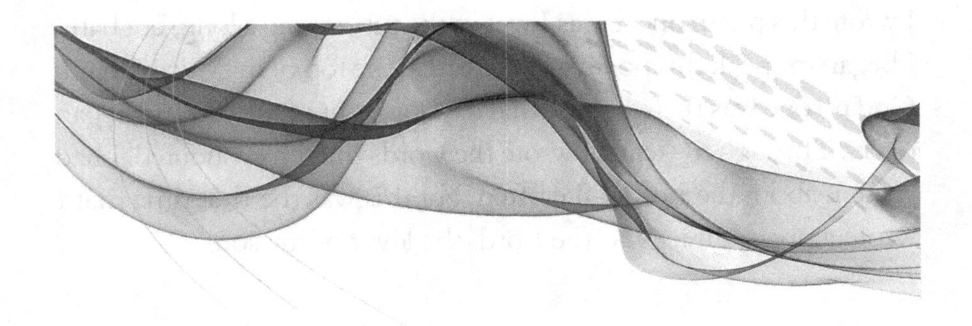

Chapter 9 Words of Love

Key to Empowerment: Gratitude

Songs, poems, books, movies, and plays have been written about love throughout the ages. As a matter of fact, the Bible is essentially a love story about God's love for His creation, humankind. I write about love in all of my books because I write about God. God is love, and there is no greater force than love. I am one who loves to love, and I love deeply. Love is a gift from God, and I have found love in many differing ways throughout my life—but the greatest is my love for Christ. I love Him because He first loved me. Christ taught me the meaning of love and how to love Him, others, and myself. For that, I am grateful. The poems in this chapter are about many facets of love.

I wrote this poem one day as I was in the tub, taking a long, hot bath. I began to speak this poem to the Lord at the top of my voice. Thank God no one was there but me that day. I got out of the tub and began to cry. Through my tears, I wrote the words that I had shouted. I had written about the Lord quite often, but this was the first time that I wrote a poem directly to the Lord, the lover of my soul.

You Are

You are the beat of my heart,

The blink of my eye,

The tears that I cry;

You are the air that I breathe,

The hope that I need,

The sweat that runs down my brow.

Sometimes I look around at all of the love and ask the question, How Could someone love me so truly, the way that you do?

It makes me want to shout and run and tell all of the world what a beautiful pearl you are.

You are the air that I breathe, the love that I need, and the one who makes me whole;

You are the issues of life, the essence of love, the one who floods my soul.

I love you. How could I ever repay day after day of bliss?

My only regret is this: the time that was lost and the moments that we missed.

I will love you throughout eternity.

I have shared the poem "Marriage" at several weddings, including my daughter's wedding and my second wedding. It captures the craziness of love that happens when you are in love and your emotions are magnified. I wrote it during a time in my life when I was in a relationship and trying to understand all the contrasting feelings of love.

Marriage

It's like honeybees and blueberries with the sun shining bright in the night.

It's like summertime and nursery rhymes with the sun shining bright in the day.

It's like feelings lost and found on a merry-go-round spinning out of control.

Nobody told me that it would be like rain in the night, with your heart squeezed tight, singing songs of rejoicing and praise.

Lollypops and spinning tops, roses with thorns and cactuses with horns, living and loving where two become one.

Oh what fun—parades in the street, dancing to the beat of your heart as it plays in my head.

Nobody said that it would be the last and the first, the best and the worst, the ultimate thirst fulfilled!

It's like strawberries and bumblebees with Christ shining bright in the day and the night.

It's like loving hard while thanking God for the one created to walk with you

Through the thick and the thin, until the very end of life as we know it right now.

"I Remember" is a poem about the intimate times that I have spent with the Lord in prayer. I know it seems as though I am talking about another human being, but I am actually talking about times spent with Christ.

I Remember

Memories flood my heart with images of times gone by.

It makes me want to cry to feel the reasons why life seems to pass me by.

Memories of days of rest while lying on your chest, melting in your arms, far away from harm's way.

The warmth of your touch, the love in your eyes, the feeling of surprise as grace melts with sin, helping me to begin again and again.

Memories flood my mind, thinking of a time when hope was at the door, begging me for more of what life has to offer.

Thank you for the memories of times past and times to be.

The memories make me free to believe in possibilities.

They bring me to my knees, anticipating, waiting, listening, and remembering you.

I wrote “A Mother’s Love” for my mother and sent it to her in a bottle for Mother’s Day one year. She really loved it, and I can still see her smiling as I recited it to her. My mother has since gone on to be with the Lord. Now I have that same gift bottle with the poem that I sent to her years ago. It’s bittersweet to think of my mother, who sacrificed so much for me and prayed for me all of my life, but especially when I was addicted to drugs. My mother’s identical twin sister once told me that I was going to kill my mother because her heart couldn’t bear the way that I lived. I know God used my mother’s love to pull me out of some of the darkest seasons of my life, and I am very grateful to her. I now try to extend that same love to my daughter Janar.

A Mother’s Love

A mother’s love is sent from above,

Created by God to show how it’s done.

It nurtures, it heals, it covers, and it fills;

It possesses and caresses,

Just like the one and only begotten Son.

It is unconditional love that is sent from above

From God our Father, who is also a Mother.

The closest thing that I have ever seen

To the real deal of love that is like none other

Is manifested in God in the person of a mother.

Communication is very important to a good relationship. When you are truly in love with someone, you desire to talk with that person all the time. I wrote "Can We Talk?" during a season of my life when God used someone to help me through a rough patch. It's good to be able to communicate love even when you aren't speaking.

Can We Talk?

Can we talk until the wee hours of the morning and until the sun begins to peep upon the horizon?

Can we talk until light becomes dark and dark becomes light?

Can we talk morning, noon, and night, even when we aren't saying a word?

Can we talk until life becomes clear and time stands still?

Can we talk through the pain and the shame until we reach down so deep that we touch the stars?

Can we talk? Can we talk? Can we talk?

Can we talk until we run out of words to say and our heartbeats speak and our knees grow weak and we create a new language of love?

Can we talk just for fun until we become one?

Can we talk? Can we talk? Can we talk?

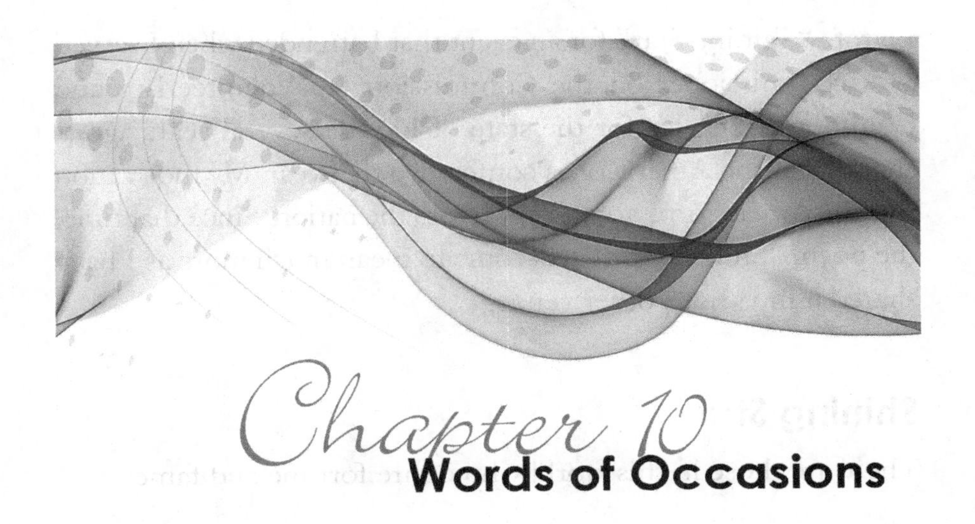

Chapter 10 Words of Occasions

Key to Empowerment: Enthusiasm

On several occasions, I was asked to write a poem for a particular event and then read the poem at the event. These opportunities proved to be very rewarding because I was able to add value and share the essence of the events in very unique ways utilizing poetry. In this chapter, I will share several poems written for such events as well as other sacred occasions.

I wrote "Shining Star" for an event that I attended when I served as a commissioner on the Commission for Volunteerism and Community Service for the state of Florida several years ago. I shared it at the AmeriCorps conference that year. My motivation was the AmeriCorps volunteers across the nation. Since that time, the poem "Shining Star" has come to mean much more as I have shared it in various other venues.

Shining Star

There are those in this world who desire fortune and fame;

They want everyone to know and say their names.

"I want to be a star" is the mantra of the day.

An obsession with their work and their play is what we see each and every day.

Day after day, we are bombarded through the media: television, radio, video, internet, newspapers, and magazines;

The same old names and faces show up on the scene.

I have lived long enough to know and realize, as I look into the eyes of our future,

That it's not about money, fortune, or fame. And who really cares who knows your name

If you don't take time to help someone along the way? To me, that is the order of the day.

The true stars are those who give money and time.

When you help others, then you really shine bright as the morning on a hot summer's day.

Keep on shining as you help others along the way.

Your reward is coming and is already here as others are blessed just because you care.

I was asked by a nonprofit organization to write a poem about local trailblazing women who were the first to work in traditionally male areas. "It Takes One to Know One" was received very positively at the event, and I really enjoyed sharing it.

It Takes One to Know One

Women who are first are women who thirst for water that has never been tasted.

So many hopes and dreams wasted while we waited for others to step up and take their places.

Women who are first are women who dare to say, "I can. So what if I am not a man? I'm well able to take a stand and command all of life to bow down to my grace and power as I bring curves and brains, pumps and earrings upon the scene."

Women who are first are women who often bear the brunt of bad jokes, bad policy, and bad breath breathing hatred and discrimination like a dragon.

Women who are first are often treated last. But this too shall pass as we move to the head of the class on the backs of women who came before us and paved the way for today and tomorrow.

Women who are first are women who thirst for all that life has to offer. Take a drink and another and another, trailblazer, mother, wife, friend, fire chief, clergy, politician, electrician, sister girl, pioneer—cheers! Here's to you, and you, and you: may all your dreams come true—to all the women who are first!

It takes one to know one.

I wrote "I Hear the Sound" for a human services conference attended by professionals from nonprofit agencies. I shared it during the luncheon. As the attendees listened attentively, I saw tears in many of their eyes as I demonstratively shared the poem. I was later told by some of the participants that the words of the poem brought hope that our coming together would indeed make a difference.

I Hear the Sound

The sound of the train as it goes across the tracks, the sound of sirens screeching in the distance, Even the sound of thunder and lightning cannot stop the voices of those crying out for help.

I hear the voices of children, women, and men asking for assistance in my head;

I hear the voices of people running scared.

I put my hand over my ears and close my eyes;

To my surprise, instead of cherries blossoming, magnolias blooming, or pearls and laces,

I see the faces of homeless children, women abused, men laid off,

People on drugs looking for love but getting slapped instead.

I speak the mantra, "As long as there is breath in your body, there is hope!" over and over again. As long as there is breath in your body, there is hope! As long as there is breath in your body, there is hope!

Hope appears when I open my eyes and see people coming together to grow and to know.

Now the voices are quieted, and I hear the sound of cleansing rain and wind blowing in a fresh new day.

This is a call and response poem that I wrote for another awards event for a local nonprofit organization. Their theme was the year of the woman. I had lots of fun with this poem because this was the first call and response poem that I had ever written.

Year of the Woman

Women's history is the history of mankind, because everyone comes from the woman's womb; and from the womb to the tomb, women have proven to be movers, shakers, and history makers.

Open wide your ears, and tell me—what do you hear?

Therefore, we know women can be anything. Just look at Hillary Clinton, former Secretary of State. She may one day be our president—we will all just have to wait.

Women can be anything that their hearts dream to be.

Women can run countries, states, cities, and still run their families.

Open wide your ears, and tell me—what do you hear?

Women can be anything. Just look around the world, and you will see how women have moved from places of obscurity into places of victory in science, business, politics, and technology.

Prominence and power hope for the hour—the hand that rocks the cradle is the one that rules the world. You go, girl!

Open wide your ears, and tell me—what do you hear?

Keep on keeping on, and let your voices be heard loud and proud from Washington, DC to Kentucky, from Florida to California, and everywhere in between.

Let it be declared as well as seen that which to me is abundantly clear.

Open wide your ears so that all can hear that this is indeed your year.

Christmas is one of my favorite holidays of all time because of its meaning. When I was growing up, I always looked forward to Christmas as a time to get gifts and be home from school. It was a time of family, food, and fun. It wasn't until I was born again that I really began to understand that the true meaning of why we celebrate Christmas is the birth of our Lord and Savior, Jesus Christ. Once I knew, I began to experience Christmas on a whole different level. It was no longer about gift giving and receiving; it became about remembering the birth of Jesus. I often ask people, "Whose birthday are we celebrating—ours, or Jesus'?" If they say Jesus, I say, "Well, He is the one who should get the gifts then, because it is His birthday." I wrote "Christmas Time" to remind us that Jesus is the reason for the season.

Christmas Time

From mistletoe to Santa's "Ho, ho, ho,"

From Rudolph's shining red nose to stocking hose,

From riding through the snow in a one-horse open sleigh to looking intently and waiting for Christmas Day—

These are the images that come into play when I think of the culture of Christmas.

The culture of Christmas is perpetuated throughout all time.

Instead of thinking of Jesus' birth, we are told to buy the next hot item to show our worth.

When will we learn that it's not about things, but it is truly about the King of kings?

Jesus came to save a dying world;

Although many didn't know it, He is indeed the pearl of great price.

So let's not stop at what we see, but let us think twice and look into history of how a virgin gave birth to the Savior of the world.

Let us continue to lift His name on high and proclaim peace and good will toward you and me

Until one day, all shall see that Jesus is the reason for the season.

My second favorite holiday is Easter, or Resurrection Sunday. Growing up, I thought this holiday was all about colored eggs, candy, and the Easter bunny. After I was born again, I realized that it is really about the death, burial, and resurrection of our Lord and Savior, Jesus Christ. I wrote "If There Is No Resurrection" based upon 1 Corinthians 15. I have recited it during many of my Resurrection Day sermons.

If There Is No Resurrection

If there is no resurrection, then why are we here?

If there is no resurrection, then all hope is gone.

If there is no resurrection, then we might as well go home.

If there is no resurrection, then Christ died in vain.

If there is no resurrection, then nothing has changed;

We are still lost in our sins, decaying, dying, and waiting for the end of a miserable life.

"Not so," I heard the Holy Ghost say.

There is a resurrection, and Jesus paved the way.

As a seed in the ground, He was planted for our sins;

But He rose on the third day for new life to begin—

A life filled with love that is Spirit-led.

Now we can receive that same resurrection power that raised Christ from the dead.

Chapter 11 Words of World Travel

Key to Empowerment: Global Thinking

We often get so caught up in what is happening in our own little worlds that we forget we are a part of a big global network that includes millions of people. In recent years, boundaries have collapsed due to the connectivity of the nternet. Today you can connect with people thousands of miles away via video, social media, e-mails, and mobile phones in a matter of minutes. We all have benefitted in various ways from our ability to more easily connect with the rest of the world.

Unfortunately, there are those who use this ability to connect to bring evil in major ways that we've never experienced before. This evil comes in the form of scams and recruitment to join violent terrorist organizations. Therefore, we must be, "Wise as serpents and harmless as doves," as it says in Matthew 10:16 (KJV), because we are becoming a more global society each day.

Several years ago, I desperately wanted to visit the continent of Africa. It became a burden to me. One day, in the middle of preaching, I began to talk about going to Africa, even though that wasn't the topic of my sermon. This touched one of my members so much that she tried to start a fund to send me to Africa. That didn't quite work out, but God did open a door for me to travel to east Africa not long after that. I went to several countries in east Africa—Nairobi, and Kisumu, Kenya, Burundi; and Kigali, Rwanda—in 2009 on a ministry trip. I was tremendously impacted by the people I met and the ministry that took place in each of the countries that we visited.

Right before landing in Nairobi after traveling for days, I was overwhelmed by God's powerful presence and wrote "The Motherland."

The Motherland

I can hear the sound of the beat of the drums in the atmosphere, even in the airplane—

The beat of a people with passion too deep for words and pain that leaves one speechless and without air to breathe.

I sense the zeal of a people with nothing to lose but everything to gain; and as they call on Jesus' name, He takes away the pain.

I know my life will never be the same, even though my feet have not yet touched African soil; the Holy Spirit met me in the air, and I do declare that I am home!

I titled this poem "Lost Luggage" because I didn't receive my two enormous suitcases of clothes when I arrived in Nairobi. We went back and forth to the airport to no avail. In fact, I didn't receive my luggage until months after traveling back from Africa to the United States. I am told that it is a miracle that I got them back. While in Nairobi, we participated in a crusade in a very large outdoor park. There were thousands of people who filled the park. As a local pastor prayed, people began acting out and were thrown onto the stage where we were standing. We were then asked to pray for them. Some of the people looked and acted like the little girl in the movie *The Exorcist.* Even though it was startling at first, we prayed for them and showed them the love of Christ. Many were set free that night!

Lost Luggage

Welcome to Kenya, a country of greatness—busy, friendly, with internet and modern rooms.

A time to pray and listen for what is to come later:

Crusade!

Swarms of people filled the park; in the midst of it all, a very dark presence came on the stage—

People acting out and souls possessed, in distress, fighting, crawling, and crying.

There we stand, in command of the powers of darkness.

Don't come near; no time for fear as devils are cast out and scurrying about.

We plead the blood, and then comes the love of God.

Hugging, sighing, crying, slain, and coming up in Jesus' name, Nairobi!

After Nairobi, we took an airplane the size of a crop duster to Kisumu. Kisumu is where President Barack Obama's paternal grandmother lived. We actually drove by her house. It was a very humble abode that had recently been renovated. Kisumu was the opposite of Nairobi in that it was very primitive. Its people didn't have many modern facilities. We stayed in the one nice gated hotel that was located in the heart of the village.

In the wee hours of the morning, we heard dogs barking and drums beating. I was told that they were having some kind of religious rituals during the night in which spirits were cast into the dogs. I didn't see it, but the night felt very foreboding. We also slept under a mosquito net each night, which was a first for me. On one night in particular, I could not sleep, so I got up and began to walk the floor and pray. I heard the dogs barking and drums beating in the distance. At one point, the porch light behind our room went out, and I felt a very dark presence. I don't know what happened to the light, but I continued to pray until morning. After that night, it was peaceful for the most part.

Obama's Village

In the bush,

In the wild,

Under the net—

Dogs barking,

Drums beating,

The Holy Spirit hovering:

Clash between good and evil.

Victory came,

Never the same—

Kisumu, Africa!

While in Burundi, we stayed in a villa with other ministers from Africa. Each night, I saw the moon shining brightly in my window. It reminded me of home and kept me connected to the familiar. The people spoke French, and the villa's cook prepared our meals fresh each day. One morning, when I went to the kitchen, I saw a live chicken clucking around the room. Later that night, after service, the cook had prepared a wonderful meal including chicken. I looked in the kitchen and did not see the chicken from that morning, and I looked at the plate of chicken prepared. For some reason, I could not bring myself to eat the chicken that night.

The Moon in My Window

The melodic sound of the French language spoken fluently and passionately,

The polite and pleasant smiles and nods—

Bon appétit, indeed!

The food so fresh until you taste the essence of flavor

As you savor every morsel of fresh pineapples, rice and beans, fish and chicken just killed—

Have your fill!

A place where God is magnified,

A place of joy,

A place of pride—Burundi!

We traveled by bus to Kigali from Burundi. As we traveled around the hills, we were stopped several times by armed guards. When I asked why they were stopping the bus, I was told that they were looking for bribes. Fortunately, we were not detained. I have heard stories of others being detained and even jailed for no reason.

The hills of Rwanda were very breathtaking to behold. Kigali is the capital and the largest city of Rwanda. It reminded me of any big city in the United States. While I was in Rwanda, I met several of the hotel staff that had family members who were killed during the genocide that took place there in the 1990s. Many were left orphans.

One young man in particular was Emmanuel. He really touched my heart as I heard his story. We have kept in touch via Facebook over the years. I also visited the Kigali Memorial Centre while in Rwanda. I was visibly moved by the skulls of those murdered and the pictures of the children slaughtered because of the tribal war. As I was leaving the museum, I was asked to recite a poem. I shared "Where Is Hope?" on the steps of the museum.

After leaving Rwanda, I cried all the way back to Nairobi on the airplane. I know the people around me must have wondered what was wrong with me, but I couldn't help myself. My heart went out to the families of the slain. They told me that the memories of what happened to their loved ones would haunt them throughout eternity.

A Thousand Hills

Rwanda, the country of a thousand hills—

Around and around the mountains as we make our way to the city of tears sown during the years of genocide.

One million died!

Restoration is taking place;

You can see the light of hope on the face of one who survived the worst.

He is now looking ahead for the best in spite of the mess of the past.

Rwanda, Rwanda, God is near. Have no fear; He does hear your cries.

You will never be the same as you call on the name that is above every name.

Jesus loves you, Kigali!

On my first trip to South Africa in 2013, we stopped in Dubai, stayed overnight, and caught a connecting flight the next day. I was unexpectedly blessed by Dubai. The hot desert weather was strangely appealing to me. This was also the first time that I had been to a country whose citizens spoke Arabic as their primary language. It was actually a wonderful experience. I wrote this poem while sitting in the airport, waiting on our flight.

Connection

Dubai—oh my, how time does fly

In with a whirlwind, out after a long night.

Desert sands,

Heat like a sauna,

Gold, big, bold—

Language that unfolds like the sound of a cello;

Nice and mellow, rolls off the tongue like waves on an ocean,

Feeling the motion pouring like lotion over my ears.

Dubai, oh why did the time fly by?

Next time around, we will see the town.

Atlantis, here we come!

On my next trip to South Africa in 2014, I was on a book tour for the release of *What Is It?* My husband and I stayed for three weeks. I preached every night of the tour in churches, schools, conferences, and civic centers from Richard's Bay to Cape Town. It was a very rich experience for both of us, as we saw miracles occur. People were saved, healed, and filled with the Holy Spirit in big and small churches alike.

I lost my voice during the tour, and I even got sick. But I continued to minister every night, and the Lord moved mightily. We met wonderful people along the way, and I will always remember this experience as one of the greatest in my career. Every night, I ministered in poetry, and the people were unabashedly blessed. It was powerful to behold!

South Africa Proud

When I traveled to the continent of Africa thrice and in South Africa twice,

I learned the rhythm of the Spirit, the power of God. I can still hear it deep in my heart, and I can feel it:

The openness of those who are near it makes me proud!

Proud to be a servant of the Most High, willing to fight and not afraid to die for the Lord;

Proud to be in the family of Christ, joined with others who are Spirit nice, loving the Lord and of one accord.

From Richard's Bay to Durban and then Cape Town, we experienced the explosion and heard the sound of God's remnant preparing for the big showdown that is soon to come—

The time when our Lord comes back again to gather His bride to be by His side forever and ever.

Until then, we wait and congregate as we expand the kingdom of God.

South Africa, South Africa, keep your finger on the pulse of the things that matter; no matter how it appears, just remember that you are set free by Jesus Christ, and whom the Son sets free is free for life!

So there is no need to fear or fret; the God we serve will never forget the love and kindness that you bestowed. The half of it has not been told; as you seek, you will find it's more precious than gold.

From the bishops, the pastors, the apostles, the evangelists, the psalmists, the musicians, the servants, the members, the women, the children, the families, the gentlemen, the churches, the schools, the youth programs, the radio stations, the hotels and the homes, the cooked meals, the restaurants, the malls, the gifts, and the Rand—

In sickness and in health, God was in command, and the glory of the Lord filled every woman and man as we were casting out devils, healing the sick, saving souls, cleansing and making whole.

South Africa, South Africa, you have found your it.

So stay in the Lord, and never quit.

Remain under the glory cloud, South Africa proud!

My husband, Kwame, and I traveled with Dr. Patricia Bailey Ministries to Turkey in 2015. We toured the refugee camps filled with families who fled for their lives from Syria. I distinctively remember the babies—big, beautiful, and crying because their gums were sore from teething. It was heart-wrenching to hear the mothers ask us for something to help ease their babies' pain.

On one part of the mission, we stayed with a young husband and wife who had to flee Iran when they accepted Jesus Christ as their Lord and Savior. We also met a young mother who left her family and son in Iran because of the religious persecution of Christians. When we arrived at her home to render service, I was immediately drawn to a sign on her wall that said "There Is Hope." I knew that I was in the right place.

I was privileged to share the poem "Where Is Hope?" with them and to minister through poetry in several of the house churches. This trip really opened my eyes to the suffering of Christians all around the world. This is a poem written to the persecuted church in Turkey with love.

Yes, Lord

Jesus sees, and He knows the struggle, the pain, and the shame in claiming the name that is above all names.

He sees your anguish and hears your cry as you wonder why it has to be this way.

But just as many who came before you believed in a brighter day, another way to live and say that Jesus is the way, the truth, and the light,

You too must fight the good fight of faith as you wait and meditate on God's Word.

May His peace, love, and grace fill the place with His glory resting on each face as you praise Him and run the race that is set before you.

Also know that your brothers and sisters are standing with you, praying and believing for you to do well because the gates of hell will not prevail against you!

Turkey, Turkey, a gathering place for the broken and wounded souls fleeing for their lives, refugees on their knees, praying for relief.

God sees, and He knows. And He says to those who will go, "Feed my sheep, and be restored." And we say, "Yes, Lord!"

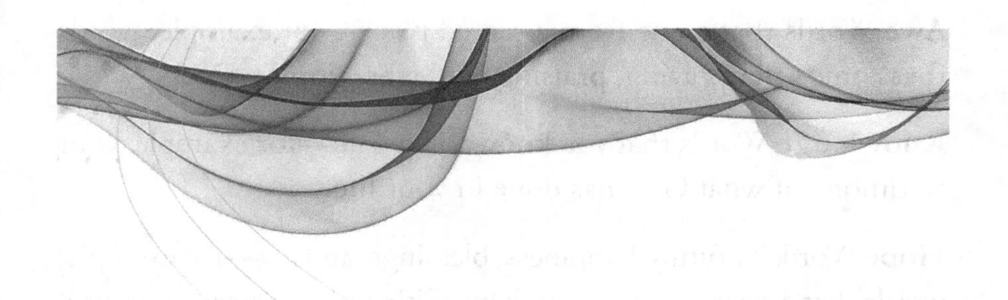

Chapter 12
Keys to Empowering

In order to use the empowerment keys identified in the previous chapters to unlock nimble anointed words, you must use powerful words. Powerful words come from the spirit within and elicit emotions in others. They allow you to make connections with people and are remembered long after conversations have ended. Powerful words are creative and add value to any situation. Although they are not always welcomed or received, they can unite and persuade because they are love-filled. Powerful words are needed words, but unfortunately, they are few and far between.

Nimble anointed words are powerful words of action. They are words that move those who read and hear them deep inside their hearts to feel differing emotions and, in some cases, take action. Below is a list of explanations for the empowerment keys identified in the book. When you use these empowering words in your writing and speaking, you will see great results in your ability to communicate and make meaningful connections with your audience.

Awe Words that come from a sacred place—for example, words that come after praying, praising, and worshipping God.

Knowledge Words that you know to be true—for example, your testimony of what God has done in your life.

Hope Words of future happiness, blessings, and joy—for example, words that give you a reason to have faith and believe in the Lord.

Resilience Words of courage to get back up when you fall, words of overcoming and bouncing back—for example, words that show why you should never give up.

Dream, Dream Big, and Dream Again Words of seeing and believing in a better world, Words of putting dreams and visions into action—for example, words that uncover and reveal dreams and visions.

Servant's Heart Words of humility and helping others—for example, words that come from a broken and compassionate place.

Creativity Words of life, words that are productive and fruitful—for example, words that come from spending time in inspirational places such as nature.

Awareness Words of who you are and who you are becoming, Words of truth based upon your life and experience—for example, decreeing words of truth.

Gratitude Words of thanksgiving or love—for example, expressing love through your words.

Enthusiasm Words of energy and purpose—for example, words that are motivated by a particular event or occasion.

Global Thinking Words of other nations and cultures—for example, words that share different cultural experiences.

Printed in the United States
By Bookmasters